MATHEMATICS FOR THE MAJORITY

ASSIGNMENT SYSTEMS

MATHEMATICS FOR THE MAJORITY

ASSIGNMENT
SYSTEMS

§

CHATTO & WINDUS
LONDON
FOR
The Schools Council

1970

Published by
Chatto & Windus (Educational) Ltd.
42 William IV Street
London W.C.2

*

Clarke, Irwin & Co. Ltd.
Toronto

ISBN 0 7010 0456 8

Printed in Great Britain by
Robert MacLehose & Co. Ltd.
The University Press
Glasgow

Contents

Note

Readers may care to refer to the specimen cards in Part 2 while they are reading Part 1. As is emphasised in the introduction to these, no perfection is claimed for the cards, either individually or as groups. They are shown as a collection which brings out varieties of content and design, and which suit different purposes and different people. Discussion about them, in the context of a reader's own circumstances, may prove to be the most valuable purpose that they can serve.

Mathematics for the Majority

The Schools Council Project in Secondary School Mathematics (now called *Mathematics for the Majority*) was set up to help teachers construct courses for pupils of average and below-average ability that relate mathematics to their experience and provide them with some insight into the processes that lie behind the use of mathematics as the language of science and as a source of interest in everyday things.

Members of the Project Team (1967–70):

P. J. Floyd (Director)
K. C. Bonnaud
T. M. Murray Rust
E. T. Norris
Mrs J. Stephens
Mrs M. J. Talbot (to 1969)
P. Kaner (Evaluator)

The chief author of this book is:

T. M. Murray Rust

Part 1
THE WHY, WHAT AND HOW OF ASSIGNMENT SYSTEMS

1

Context and Background

1. Pupil Involvement As full an involvement as possible of the pupil in his own process of learning is fundamental to the planning and practice of this Project. This is implicit throughout the Project's books. It reflects a conviction that, while personal involvement, as distinct from the mere acceptance of instruction, is desirable for pupils of any age or ability, it is vital for 'our pupils' if their interest and co-operation in learning are to be aroused and maintained.

How is this to be achieved? This is the essential theme of this book. The traditional method (and let no one underrate its success for the purposes it set out to achieve on behalf of its pupils) has emphasized the role of the teacher as a provider of the proper knowledge to be absorbed by his pupils. This was consolidated by methods at any rate akin to rote-learning, and the skills involved were acquired by the constant practice of exercises, often of a repetitive type. The subject matter was largely regulated by the examination syllabuses for which the abler pupils were preparing. Whether this was or was not the best way for older and abler pupils to be taught is not part of the Project's brief. There is plenty of evidence, however, to suggest that it is not a way which is widely successful in involving our pupils in their mathematical work. What alternatives are presented? Here the primary school experience cannot be ignored. In the past traditional methods, akin to those of secondary schools, were practised — also under a shadow cast by an examination system relevant only to the needs of the able children. The shadow is disappearing and the methods are largely discarded, for able and less able children alike, in favour of a group-working organisation involved in a discovery approach. The planning, presentation and follow-up use of assignments, in some form or other, is a major part of the work and the responsibility of the teacher involved in such an approach, and this is the justification for a consideration here of the possibilities and implications of an assignment system in the context of our pupils.

2. Primary School Development A close study of primary school development is clearly necessary because the previous learning of our pupils is most relevant to our own plans on their behalf at the age at which they come to us. A further reason, however, for such a study may well lie in the possibility that methods found acceptable and profitable with younger children will throw considerable light on methods worth trying with less able older pupils.

There is abundant literature, available in teachers' libraries whether in schools or in teachers' centres, describing the ideas and achievements of child-involved methods of learning mathematics in primary schools, and secondary teachers would be well advised to consult some of this. The Mathematical Association's report on the teaching of mathematics in primary schools has close links with its report dealing with mathematics in secondary modern schools. The Schools Council's publication 'Mathematics in Primary Schools: Curriculum Bulletin No. 1' not only covers the work in primary schools but points the way to continuity of learning through to the secondary stage. Essentially such work is based on a belief in the value of the 'discovery approach' to the pupil's learning. This approach is by no means new, and discovery methods, of one sort or another, have been practised for a very long time at the hands of imaginative teachers.

3. 'Spiral' Progression This type of approach has involved a change in attitude to syllabus-progression. It is now realised that, in the course of widespread experience of his environment and its needs, a pupil will come across the need for a broad variety of mathematical ideas and, thence, of skills. These ideas will not be met once and for all, at some specific stage in the syllabus; they will be met again and again, at successive stages of age and maturity, and they will demand increasingly sophisticated skills. Again, there is nothing new in this spiral or concentric conception of the progressive acquisition of learning and knowledge; it happens to be the one that is intimately connected with a discovery approach.

4. Class Organisation This approach compels a re-consideration of the organisation of a whole class (or form or set) as an undivided unit for teaching purposes. The belief that a sub-division into groups must be envisaged is inherent in primary school practice and has already led to similar patterns of organisation in secondary school experiments. In this context it may be strongly urged that the individual teacher's discretion to conduct the teaching of his class in ways that he considers to their best advantage must continue. There may be times at which he considers it best for his pupils to be learning individually — but let it be assumed that the obvious value of their working 'at their own pace' does involve their working 'at their own *best* pace'. There may be times, on the other hand, when the size of the teaching group is the whole class, or a substantial part of it. Experience suggests that, for much of their time, the pupils work in small groups of 2, 3 or 4. This permits a healthy discussion of their work by the pupils themselves which is inhibited when the group is either individual or large. How to organise the groups, perhaps according to the ability of the pupils, perhaps according to the equipment and furniture available, perhaps according to the chosen method of involving the pupils

4

in their work and so on, remains the responsibility of the teacher concerned, and different views will be held on the various problems involved in this.

2

Aspects of an Assignment System

1. Aims and Objectives An assignment system, like any other system, does not come into operation in a vacuum but must be preceded by an adequate consideration of its aims and objectives, and of the purposes to be served by it.

It cannot be emphasised too strongly that such a system does not consist of involving the pupil in a sequence of unrelated tasks. This does not, of course, rule out the great merits of lines of learning that appear to the pupil to have arisen spontaneously. Many will genuinely have done so. Others, however, will seem to have done so, although the teacher has in fact contrived the situation that gave rise to them. All lines of·learning should take their place within the framework of objectives planned by the teacher.

General Aims The 'Dalton Plan' in time past, not always well understood or implemented even by its exponents, was sometimes caricatured as a system under which pupils were kept employed (ostensibly quiet) in 'doing what they liked' with the teacher being little, if at all, in evidence. From such experience an assignment system did not always acquire a good name. Actually much devoted and successful work has been achieved unobtrusively, whether specifically under this 'Plan' or in ways which carried through similar beliefs in 'pupil-involvement'. Such work laid foundations for what are now claimed as desirable and attainable objectives in assignment working. These would include the provision of varied and abundant opportunities for the pupils to exercise their powers of intuition and imagination. They would discuss their work, both among themselves and with their teacher. They would form judgments and make decisions. They would execute these decisions with all the mathematical tools and skills at that time at their disposal. And they would record their results and findings in such ways as they themselves and others may find suitable for subsequent interpretations. The objectives would also envisage a genuine sharing (*not* a transfer) of responsibility for work and learning between teacher and pupil.

Specific Objectives Assignments can be devised deliberately to meet various teaching requirements and they can be considered as having their main emphasis under one or other of two categories. On the one hand the assignments may be directed towards specific objectives. Such an objective might be practice in computation; or it might be the spread of application of a concept just grasped by the pupil; or the spread

6

of application of a skill or technique just acquired; or a lead-in to a new concept or technique. Certain definite results would be expected by the teacher from the operation of this type of assignment, and its success would be judged on the extent to which these were achieved. But teachers very soon realise that the success of what they planned may be conditioned by circumstances of pupil and period; what works with one pupil at one time may appear less successful at others, while success in unexpected directions sometimes materialises.

Open-ended Objectives The second category is what is popularly described as 'open-ended' — a description open to much misunderstanding and not at all easy to define. In essence, it involves a pupil being confronted with a problematic situation and he is left with the responsibility of appraising it, of realising its implications in mathematical terms, of planning methods for its solution (or, in some cases, for investigation when solution is not obtainable) and for recording and interpreting his conclusions. Such a prospect may seem at first sight woolly, wasteful of time, not serving such valuable purposes as could be achieved by more specific direction and guidance, and so on. Nevertheless, experience of this type of assignment does offer evidence of really concrete values and achievements. It helps to develop in the pupils qualities of observation and enquiry, of planning and decision-making, of communication and interpretation of the end-products of a task, to each other and to the teacher. A side benefit is the quantity and quality of sheer computation which the pupils produce to serve their needs.

An Appendix to Part I of this book is devoted to a study of open-ended questioning.

Value in Variety There is, however, no need for a teacher embarking on an assignment system to feel that he must give his entire allegiance to one or other of these categories. Some needs may, at his discretion, be best served by one type of assignment, other needs by another. It would be a pity if it were dogmatically believed (and there has been a risk of this) that the open-ended category is the first-class brand to which a teacher will aspire after experience, shorter or longer, of the second-class, directed, type. On the other hand it may be claimed that the pupils will not have been offered the full advantages of an assignment system unless their opportunities include some considerable experience of dealing with open-ended situations. A teacher who may be understandably hesitant to embark on open-ended situations, or who does not quite see his way how to do it, may find a clue to his dilemma in some of the less expected results of purpose-directed assignments, when the pupils have seized on open-ended possibilities lurking behind the intended guide lines.

2. Assignments and Organisation As suggested above a flexible organisation of groups within the class seems to be called for. Various alternatives are possible in the formation of these groups, and such alternatives need not be mutually exclusive — sometimes one arrangement may be, in the teacher's view, the most suitable, sometimes another. The grouping may be on a basis of more or less homogeneous ability; or it may deliberately seek a cross-section of abilities within the group; or it may be a 'friendship' grouping taken up by the pupils themselves. Each alternative has its claims to advantage and its risks of abuse, and over a period of time a class may in fact have used all of them. Individual personalities may well influence the teacher's preference for one or the other.

Another influence may be the school's system of organisation — e.g. streamed or unstreamed, with or without setting for mathematics. Some schools are experimenting with team-teaching, when, for at any rate part of their mathematical time, forms from the same age group do their work simultaneously and possibly in the same place (e.g. an assembly hall) or in neighbouring rooms. The teachers concerned act as a team and involve themselves in the pupils' work irrespective of which form the pupils actually belong to. This form of experiment in organisation is at present largely limited to the first two years of secondary teaching, but it is spreading to those in our age ranges, and the Project would wish to encourage the extension of this. Some secondary schools might, in the course of time, be experimenting with vertical grouping through age-ranges (or vertical setting from a series of forms), and there would be considerable interest to be derived from the giving of assignments under such conditions.

3. Communication of Assignments. Care has been taken so far to discuss the question of assignments without any reference to cards. In various controversies which teachers are likely to meet on the subject of using or not using assignment cards, it is as well always to stress that there are alternative ways of involving the pupils in assignment work and that the choice among these rests with the teacher.

Clearly with non-readers, whether these are infants still learning to read at the normal stage or whether they are older, retarded pupils, a word-of-mouth presentation is called for. Word-of-mouth will often be the natural method of extending an assignment which was in the first place presented in script or print. For the most part, however, work to be done will be presented through the medium of the writen or printed page. This might involve text-book exercises, or it might involve a worksheet or jobcard — a written or printed assignment under some name or other. The great advantage that a card system (as we shall call it, irrespective of the type of material on which the assignments are written or printed) has over the text-book is its flexibility and its possible impermanence. The remainder of this book will be concerned with systems of assignment *cards*; but it is again stressed that such systems are certainly not exclusive of other methods of disseminating work, whether by word of mouth or by the deliberate and judicious use of a text-book.

4. Assignments Only One Way to an End. It must be emphasized again that an assignment system is not an end in itself but is just one means of promoting the pupils' best learning. To whatever extent one may be used, it does not preclude the accompanying use of other methods of teaching.

It is quite possible, however, that the teacher-pupil relationships and the classroom atmosphere (not least of ample discussion) built up when an assignment system is operated may have a beneficial and refreshing influence on the operation of other, maybe more traditional methods.

Assignment Card Systems

1. Origins of a Collection of Cards *Who composes the cards?* There can be little or no doubt that the best composer is the teacher actually concerned with the pupils who are to use them. He can frame the cards so as to serve his own needs at the teaching end and his pupils' capabilities at the receiving and learning end. No one else can do this quite as ideally as he can, though, certainly in the beginning, a teacher may not find it in practice as easy or as successful as he would like. This, however, would apply to the early stages of any teaching method; if the teacher has the will to persevere, he will assuredly find the way. Meanwhile he will hope to receive advice, encouragement and support from those with greater experience than himself.

In some schools the assignment cards used have been largely or entirely composed by one person, for example the Head of the mathematics department. This system may not have the same efficiency and personal relevance as one devised by an individual teacher for his own pupils, although different teachers operating the same set of centrally written cards have been known to produce considerable variety of response from their own particular pupils. There could be some advantage in having both systems available simultaneously. The centrally-composed cards could act as an example to an individual teacher when he sets about his own writing of cards, and this might be of particular help to a teacher inexperienced in this form of approach to his pupils' work. Furthermore a collection of such cards could be some sort of insurance against the dislocation caused by changes of staff.

A third source of assignment cards is the commercial market, and it lies with the individual teacher, the Head of department or the Head of the school to decide whether any of the sets of cards available for purchase are required at all or could serve any particular purposes (by themselves or in conjunction with cards composed on the spot).

In a somewhat different category come the assignments involved in one or other of the systems of programmed learning. These are intended, if not to dispense with the human presence of the teacher, at any rate to reduce the need for his contributions to a minimum. The composition of the assignments must be 'foolproof' — the phrasing must allow of no uncertainty in interpretation and must ensure self-checking. On the other hand the assignment card with which we are concerned in this book should be designed so as not to eliminate the teacher's influence and guidance but to complement it in co-operation with the part played by the pupils themselves. The teacher would always be available to interpret, guide and supplement.

2. **Types of Card**: *Of What Material?* In the first place, what are they to be made of? They might be work-sheets on paper, destined (by design or otherwise) for an early consignment to the waste-paper basket when they have served the specific purpose for which they were written. They are more usually made of actual card (which may be protected from defacement and decay by a plastic covering), in the belief that their use will not be limited to one operation but that they can be used again with other pupils. There are arguments for and against the short-lived and the semi-permanent types − and there may well be a place for both types to be in use simultaneously.

Forms of Assignment

What form should the actual assignment on the card take? The only possible answer to this is ... 'it just depends'. Part II will suggest some possible variations in the context in which a particular card is composed. According to this, and according to the intended purpose of the card (cf. section 1 chap. 2) the layout and appearance of the assignment will vary.

Specifically Directed? At one end of the scale it could reflect an entirely directed and restricted situation − for example it could consist of a set of text-book type of examples for drill purposes. Whereas judicious use of actual text-books might still be a better way of serving this purpose, the use of cards could be justified whether on the grounds of expense saved on the purchase of text-books or because of the possibility of drawing the examples from a variety of sources and not only from the book currently in use.

Experiments are, in fact, being made with a view to guiding the pupil towards the use of source materials, specifically including a variety of text and reference books. For such a purpose an assignment card could specifiy actual examples to be done (and passages to be consulted) from a variety of books. While this would be one method of enabling the teacher to set what were in his view the most suitable examples for a pupil, it might also prove to be a way of leading the pupil towards accepting his own responsibility in the selection and consultation of source material.

Fully Open-ended? At the other end of the scale comes the fully open-ended assignment. This will studiously avoid the least suggestion of direction in presenting the problem or situation to be confronted by the pupil, and in doing this it could fail to make it clear to the pupil what exactly he has to do. In actual fact there is little harm that can come from this as the teacher himself is available for preliminary discussion in which doubts can be cleared up. Incidentally, in seeking to allay such doubts there is often a grave temptation of saying too much, with the result of providing the direction it was hoped to avoid!

Multi-Facet? Most usually an assignment card is of a 'multi-facet' type, a description that may need explanation. The term multi-facet is commonly used to define one sort of examination question in which the candidate is given a situation out of which a number of mathematical questions are evolved; these are the facets. This sort of question figured in discussions which preceded the introduction of the Certificate of Secondary Education, on the grounds that such questions could reflect a wide variety of the work done at school by the candidates. A considerable amount of the work in secondary modern schools was already of project type, and the multi-facet questions involved project-type situations restricted enough to be dealt with under examination conditions. Each such question, if presented separately on a card, could in fact be used as a multi-facet type of assignment. To the extent that each facet poses a definite question, for a definite purpose and with a definitely intended answer, these cards are directed and not open-ended, although there is nothing to prevent a multi-facet card having open-ended facets. Examples of multi-facet and open-ended cards are given below, and more will appear in the second part of this book devoted to examples. Ideas for discussions on multi-facet cards, and possibly suggestions for compiling some, might be drawn from the examples of multi-facet questions printed in the Schools Council's Examination Bulletins No. 2 and No. 4.

Same Assignment – Different Forms of Presentation

CARD A. This is of multi-facet type, asking specific questions but giving some opportunity for the pupil's exercise of his judgement and powers of decision.

CARD B. This assignment is quite open-ended; if the teacher would like special points to be brought out and the pupil has not done so, then discussion and supplementary questions could prompt his turning his attention to them – this does not involve actually telling him.

CARD C. This sort of free-for-all open-ended assignment leads to much imagination and ingenuity on the part of the pupils – and usually to a surprising spread of mathematics.

CARD D. Another aspect of an open-ended demand on the pupil.

Note: The pie-chart given here has some special case-features. The angles are 'easy' – $30°$, $60°$, $120°$, $150°$. A pupil could notice that as much time is spent on A and D together as on B and C. A teacher could bring in the need for some more complicated computational thought and

12

A

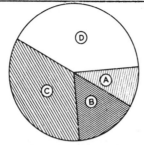

This chart shows how a boy divides up his time between arriving home at 5pm after school and going to bed at 10pm.

A represents the time spent in having his tea; B represents the time spend on homework; C represents the time spent in watching television; and D represents the time spent on all sorts of other things.

a. How long does the boy spend on each part?

b. What proportion of the total time is spent on each part?

c. If you can, use a block-graph to represent the same times spent on tea, homework and television between arrival back at 4:30pm and bedtime at 10:30pm.

d. What proportion of the total time is now spent on each part?

e. Say whether you prefer one form of diagram rather than the other, and, if so, why?

B

The same chart and description of what it refers to is given.
The assignment then reads:
Discuss possible deductions from this chart.
Discuss whether other sorts of diagram could serve the same purposes equally well or better.

C

The same chart is given, but no description of the situation.
The assignment then reads:
Devise, in as much detail as you like, a situation which could be diagrammatically represented by this chart.

D

Between arriving home from school at 1700 hours and going to bed at 2200 hours a boy spends $\frac{1}{12}$ of this time at meals, $\frac{1}{6}$ of this time doing his homework, $\frac{1}{3}$ of this time watching television and $\frac{5}{12}$ of this time doing other things. (Alternatively the number of minutes spent on each activity could be given.)

The assignment then reads:
Represent this information diagrammatically in more than one way. What are, in your opinion, the advantages and disadvantages of each method?

technique by varying the sizes of the angles. Card D might not give a detailed timing of the situation but leave it to the pupil to confess, in the diagram, how he actually spends his time!

Further variations on this theme could involve groups of pupils performing similar assignments for situations occurring on different days of the week — with the supplementary question 'are there any significant variations from day to day? If so, why?'

Equipment Lists

A list of equipment or apparatus required in the pursuit of an assignment is often written in on the assignment card. This can be very valuable to a teacher when he is planning what assignments he will be giving to which pupils. In many cases it will be valuable to the pupils in getting themselves organised, although with the more experienced pupils the added problem of selecting their own equipment will be a useful responsibility to place on them.

3. Building up an Initial Card Collection *A sufficiency of cards:* to amass enough cards to make the operation of an assignment system initially viable is a daunting prospect for a teacher about to embark on this approach for the first time. Sooner or later the back of the problem will be broken and a first collection will be achieved. Thereafter there will be plenty of card-composing to do, both to supplement and to replace those already in use, but the machine will be working; the pressure will seem less, and sources of inspiration will be enlarged by suggestions from the pupils and by further ideas that come from their response to the existing cards. The teacher may, indeed, find that, as he goes about his daily round, he is becoming increasingly observant of what goes on in his surroundings. In such a way lists of possible topics can grow. Suggestions for mathematical questions arising from them can be jotted down. And, when the time comes, there will be a collection of ideas from which actual assignments can be crystallised. This is an attitude which may also be taken up by some of the pupils, who will contribute their own ideas towards the fulfilment of a dream of a snowballing of cards.

Meanwhile, however, a start has to be made. The possibility has already been envisaged of collections of cards being available in the school, either composed centrally within the school or obtained commercially. Colleagues' collections may be offered to help out in this situation. Thus, in one way or another other peoples' cards may be used, either directly with the pupils or to give suggestions for personal composition of a teacher's own collection.

Another source of initial suggestion and help is available. The very great number of teachers who have attended courses run by Miss E. E. Biggs

14

H.M.I. (or courses run on similar lines) have been helped to start off assignment systems by the assignments tackled by themselves during the course. Appendix 3 of Curriculum Bulletin No. 1 contains a selection of such assignments which, although suitable for primary school children to deal with at their level, had been tackled by the teachers at adult level. They reflect situations which could be as relevant to secondary pupils as they were to the primary children.

How Many Cards for a Class? The number of cards needed for simultaneous use can only be decided by the teacher concerned, and will depend on how he organises his class. Will they all be doing assignment work at the same time? They well may do so eventually, but need they do so at the start of this process of card-library building? What number of pupils are there going to be in each group? Even if it were desirable on other grounds, individual working demands more cards in simultaneous use than if the groups were larger. A minimum of cards would clearly be needed if the whole class worked as a single group. A happy mean probably lies somewhere in between.

Can there be duplicate (or near-duplicate) cards? Certainly, if more groups than one may be suited by similar assignments.

An encouraging way to start a collection is, in fact, to compose an assignment card, and then to write similar cards with, say, numerical differences. Actually this device might serve to produce 'n' cards in return for one bright idea. There could be a positive advantage to be gained by the same pupils considering the same situation with different numerical data, and questions of estimation and of assessing degrees of accuracy relevant to the different cases could be introduced.

4. Controversies Strong feelings are sometimes expressed about the necessity for or desirability of having a card system at all; the pupils' response to one situation or line of research, it is claimed, will inevitably suggest what is to be done next. There is certainly evidence of this being so in the relationship between some teachers and their pupils. Nevertheless the teachers concerned will, at any rate in most cases, have graduated to this stage of relationship through previous stages when they may have relied considerably on assignment cards. There is little doubt that the transition from the exclusive use of text-books to the use of assignment cards has made possible for many teachers the adoption of a more pupil-involved relationship in their teaching; this is a step which they might have been very hesitant to take without the 'anchorage' provided by the cards. Furthermore, even those teachers who are highly experienced in this discovery approach might — who knows? — find occasion for the use of a written assignment or two. What is not at all desirable is for those teachers who are contemplating the challenging first steps in a different approach to their teaching to feel that they must take rigid sides in a controversy suggesting that cards are either 'in' or 'out' of the accepted educational scene.

Directed or Open-ended? Even if the acceptability of a card system for certain purposes under certain circumstances is granted, controversy can then rage as to the nature of the cards. Ideally, it is sometimes said, should these not always be open-ended, leaving the pupils to choose and pursue their own lines of developing the given situation? It is urged that such controversy be avoided if it is going to suggest yet another sheep/goat separation between those who include some direction of purpose in their assignments and those who are exclusively open-ended.

Good or Bad Cards? Does it not all depend on circumstances — all sorts of circumstances, human and otherwise? Sometimes, for some purposes, at the hands of some teachers, the use of assignment cards will be called for — but perhaps not always. Similarly the cards may be to some extent directed — but perhaps not always. Sometimes they may be (to some extent?) open-ended. What does matter, however, is that for whatever purpose the cards are used, and whatever the type of card, the cards shall be as good as possible. And what constitutes good cards or less good cards begs considerable questions — the first being 'is it not possible for a card to be good for some purposes and less good for others?' Any answers to such questions are bound to be subjective, and rightly so, although there may be certain types of card which need especially close scrutiny by the teacher before he decides that they are really the best for his purpose. Three such questionable types may be suggested:

(i) One in which such explicit directions are given that little or no responsibility for decision making is left to the pupil.

(ii) One which consists of a sequence of repetitive examples quite unconnected with each other except for the technique they may require.

(iii) One in which virtually all the work has been done by the teacher, leaving the pupils to make only brief answers. Under this heading would come a series of sentences with blanks for the pupils to fill in. It may be claimed that thought is necessary before the blanks are filled in; in this case, why not expect the pupils to devise a method of recording and presenting their thoughts?

5. Role of the Teacher *What is the teacher's part in such a system?* An assignment system is *not* an end in itself — a situation in which one just adopts it or one does not adopt it. As we see it, the assignment system provides a route by which the pupils become enmeshed in their work. It is when they are so enmeshed that the teacher can share their involvement and can bring his experience and his adult mind to bear on their thoughts, their problems and their achievements. The part he plays, and the influence that he can exert, may be, at any rate partially, thought of under the following headings:

16

(i) *Choice of Cards*

The selection of the cards, whether he composes them himself or whether he draws on the composition of others, is his responsibility. The cards must be designed to serve his purposes with his pupils.

(ii) *Guidance of pupils*

While the pupils are working on the assignments, his influence can be directed towards taking an active interest in them. He can provoke them (perhaps with leading questions); he can encourage them and approve of their efforts; he can lead them on to supplementary ideas by means of supplementary questions; he can help them to master or circumvent their problems and difficulties by any means short of telling them the solutions or how to achieve them. In some cases the teacher may seem to be guiding a pupil for 98% of the road to his victory; the victory will be, for such a pupil, none the less effective and encouraging if the final 2% of a 'discovery' comes from his brain and his lips.

(iii) *Assessment*

The teacher will be, consciously or largely unconsciously, assessing his pupils' progress and will be ready to suggest ways of furthering it. Such ways might involve the operation of further assignments in an already planned progressive sequence — on the other hand they might involve a supplementary assignment given on the spur of the moment by word of mouth (and very possibly added subsequently to the series of cards).

To the extent that some parts of an assignment system may have been directed towards the absorption of certain mathematical ideas or the acquiring and refining of certain techniques, familiar ways of testing progress may be employed. If available, objective tests of progress or attitude can help a teacher to confirm or reject his own views of a pupil's progress. Moreover the format in which some of his assignment work has been presented to the pupil — e.g. in multi-facet assignments — is obviously appropriate for one form of testing. The multi-facet question appearing in some external examinations is in itself an assignment of this sort being used for the purpose of testing.

(iv) *Cross fertilisation of Ideas*

If he shares his own experience and that of his pupils in this assignment work with other teachers, whether in his own school or in a teachers' centre or anywhere else, a cross-fertilisation of ideas and of possibilities can be affected. Everybody cannot have all the bright ideas all the time, and the operation of many assignment systems can be enhanced by such exchanges.

6. Conclusions Before passing on to the examples of Part II it might be valuable to set out, starkly and briefly, the types of advantage which we feel are fostered by the working of an assignment system.

Mathematical advantage: the pupil is applying his mathematical knowledge and skills to situations which he is personally concerned to unravel. He has to select his mathematical tools and he has to use them correctly. He has to interpret the mathematical implications of his researches or solutions. If his knowledge is inadequate, he welcomes the prospect of increasing it. However humble his level, he is a 'mathematical thinker', and not only a 'mathematical doer'. And, when the moment comes for him to take mathematical action the correctness and success of this does not overwhelmingly depend on memorisation.

Educational advantage: the background to his assignment experiences can be a wide one and can overflow into those of other branches of his school learning. His attitude to his mathematical assignments can fit in with — may even enhance — his general attitude to learning. Not the least valuable contribution that his assignment work can make is the development of his own responsibility for selecting and gathering together such material as he needs for the completing of a task. This may involve the collection of necessary tools; whereas in a pupil's earlier stages his assignment cards often include a list of equipment that will be required, there comes a time when such a list is omitted and the pupil himself is left to choose what equipment he needs and to get it ready for use with as little delay as possible. This personal responsibility may well involve a knowledge of sources of information which he can consult in planning how to accomplish his task. This may involve the use of printed material — and a familiarity with the use of a reference library; but it may also involve a knowledge of the right experts to consult for personal assistance, and of the right questions to ask them.

Social advantage: the responsibility taken and the confidence gained by a pupil in the course of his assignment work can also overflow into other aspects of his life and of his relationships with other people. As well as his experience of working individually on his own — 'at his own *best* pace' as urged above — he gains experience of working in partnership, of discussing with others, of arguing sensibly for his own point of view, of forming judgments and of taking (and implementing) decisions. These qualities may well stand him in good stead later on, in his home, in his employment and, indeed, as a citizen.

Appendix to Part 1
'Open-ended' Questioning

After reading the first draft of this book, a member of the Project's Consultative Committee, Mr. D. Sturgess of the University of Nottingham Institute of Education, sent in a short paper on the topic of open-ended assignments. This was supported by an extract from a story by Mr. D. Orton entitled *The Reaction of Children to Different Forms of Written Instruction*, and submitted for the Advanced Diploma in Education of Nottingham University. This seemed to be of more than sufficient interest to include as an appendix to this book, and permission to do this was obtained from Mr. Sturgess, Mr. Orton and the Director of the Institute.

In the course of Mr. Orton's study the verbal reasoning quotients (V.R.Q.) of the contributing pupils are given, and these are reflected in the quality and quantity of *written* response. Does this necessarily mean that open-ended situations are inappropriate to the less able pupils, as is often suggested? Or does it mean that from some of these pupils the teacher might invite a main response that is *not* written, but which comes from word-of-mouth, perhaps supported by diagram or apparatus?

The most significant evidence from the study comes from the references to 'many arguments', accompanied by repeated experimenting with the apparatus involved. If the pupils can be induced to dispute with each other about their mathematics, they are involved and interested and prepared to go further. The verbal accompaniment to this particular study was probably the most valuable effect of this piece of open-ended questioning. A moral can be drawn to the effect that this form of questioning should not have its outcome appraised solely by its written results.

From: Mr. D. Sturgess

A card or assignment (or verbal instruction) is open-ended, as I understand it, if there is more than one answer. The point of asking such questions is to give the pupils complete freedom to explore a situation. In this situation some pupils discover things that others have done before, but sometimes a pupil will find a completely new field to explore. The teacher has a vital role to play in this situation by asking a leading question, where one is necessary, or by following a line of exploration which is completely new to him (the teacher).

In this situation all pupils feel a degree of insecurity which is often expressed in a question like 'But what do *you* want me to do?' Pupils have to be educated to accept and use the freedom which is theirs in an open-ended context, and guided cards can help, but they can also hinder by providing a false sense of security (they tell you *what* to do!).

The best security of all is probably that provided by apparatus. A geo-board with only nine pins on it provides considerable practical restrictions; a number of card squares can only be fitted together in certain ways; a set of plastic strips (or cuisenaire rods) come in a definite number of lengths. These restrictions on the activity can make a very open-ended question possible because the number of solutions at least appears to be finite. When pupils have explored the finite possibilities of a situation they are then often quite willing to generalise and see 'What happens if . . .?'. 'I can find 6 squares on a 9-pin board, what happens if I have an $n \times n$ pin-board?'

Open-ended questions are generally very short. The first sentence is the important one, the other questions are merely suggestions for development. For example:

I. *Using Cuisenaire Rods*

Choose any two differently coloured rods from the box. Find what other lengths you can make using these and other rods of the same colour.

Will you get a different result using other colours?

Can you make a general statement that would be true whatever two colours you start with?

(All such general statements should be tested by other pupils as well as the teacher. The criterion is not 'Is it right or wrong' but 'Can we find an example to prove it wrong?')

II. *Using Plastic Strips with Holes and Paper Clips*

Make some shapes using the strips and paper clips. Make some statement which is true of all the shapes that you have made. Test whether this statement is true for some shape that you have not already made.

(This could lead to a study of rigidity, or of networks or of many other things I have not yet discovered!)

III. *Using 9-Pin and 16-Pin Geo-Boards*

How many squares can you make on the geo-board?

Are they all the same shape?

Are they all the same size?

How many can you make on a 16-pin geo-board?

What can you say about the squares that you have made that would be true for all geo-boards?

Can you guess how many squares you can make on 25 pins? Try it and see if your guess was correct.

What else could you say about squares on geo-boards?

(There are many different answers to this question. It is still possible to do the whole card quite consistently if all six squares on the 9-pin board are not discovered.)

IV. *Using Squares of Card* (all the same size)

Using only four squares how many different patterns can you make if the whole of at least one edge of each square touches the whole of an edge of another square?

What happens if you use more than four squares?

(The number of answers depends upon whether or not reflections and rotations are considered the same, whether it is considered as a problem in 2D or 3D and so on. Provided the pupil can state his premises, the answers are all correct.)

The answers to these questions can all be the starting points of discussion between the members of a group, between group and group, or teacher and pupils. In order that results can be communicated they will have to be recorded in a meaningful way.

Extract from Mr. Orton's Study:

TRIANGLES

Card 0.2 (1½ hours in two sessions)

What can you discover about making triangles with elastic bands on the 9-pin geo-board?

Each child worked individually, following his own fields of discovery, often showing the other members of the group his own particular discovery. Many arguments ensued, and the 'catch phrase' appeared to be 'Prove it'. Doreen held up ⊿ and said that this was the biggest triangle that could be made on this board. Keith, in reply, held up ∧ and asked if this one was bigger. This involved five of them, and they asked how they could find out, deciding that the only sure way was to find the areas. I showed them a 'small' square and suggested that this might be easier to use as a unit of measurement. They were able to find the area of Doreen's one easily, but with Keith's they found it difficult to count the 'bits'. Eventually, after much thought, they discovered ⊿ and expressed

21

some surprise that this indicated that the two triangles had the same area.

Ian was convinced after a lengthy argument with Clive that there were 16  and not 14 — neither could convince the other until they counted the number that could be made on each pair of pins forming the smallest side. Keith wanted to know which was bigger ⦂△ or ⦂⃫ eventually he discovered that in ⃫ the rectangle and the parallelogram had the same area, and saw at once the solution to his problem on the pair of triangles.

Freddy made lots of triangles at the same time on his board. He pointed out to me that ·⋈· made two large triangles and four small triangles, and that the space in the middle was a 'diamond' shape — *but not the same as a square turned round*.

Ian investigated the symmetry of his triangles, and a useful discussion took place with Keith and Clive about its properties and the different axes of symmetry they could see.

Such a variety of fields was explored that it would be most difficult to describe except by reproducing as faithfully as possible *each child's work*. This has been attempted. (Each child's work has not been reproduced here. Work from pupils in the top range of V.R.Q.'s has been omitted.) Comments, and the correct results when errors have been made, are placed in brackets. The spelling has been reproduced as accurately as possible.

Christine (V.R.Q. 78)

9 Triangles

4 Triangles

6 Traingles

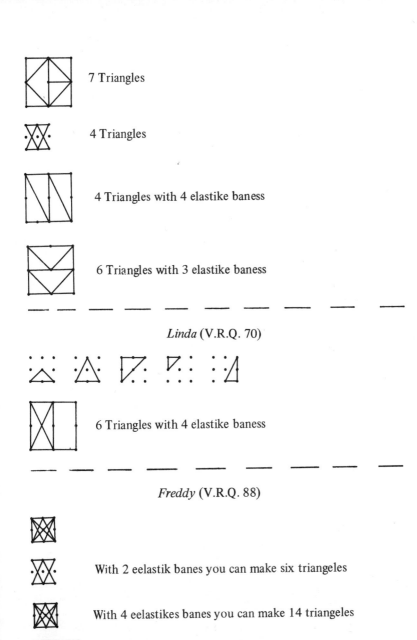

7 Triangles

4 Triangles

4 Triangles with 4 elastike baness

6 Triangles with 3 elastike baness

Linda (V.R.Q. 70)

6 Triangles with 4 elastike baness

Freddy (V.R.Q. 88)

With 2 eelastik banes you can make six triangeles

With 4 eelastikes banes you can make 14 triangeles

With 8 elastike banss you can make 28 triangeles

All triangles have three sides. There are 16 (8 types, 76 possibilities) triangles you can make on the nine-pin nail board.

These shapes are the same size which is 8 small squares.

I can find 8 (16) of these triangles on the 9 pin nail board.

This is the largest triangle and you can make it 4 times.

I can get 8 of these shapes on the 9 pin nail board. (a line omitted)

Doreen (V.R.Q. 110)

There are many different triangles you can make on the nine pin geoboard.

This is one of the largest triangle you can make on the nine pin geoboard. You can make four of these on the nine pin geoboard. This shape covers six nails. If you put two of these shapes together on upright and one upside down in the midle there will be a diomand.

There is four (16) of these on the nine pin geoboard. (See below for second thoughts).

24

These are all the same sort of square but they are in different angles.

4   16   4   15(16)

Ian (V.R.Q. 117)

This diagram covers 1½ (1) or 3 (4) squares approx. you can do it 16 times this has 1 right angle. This shape is not symetrical.

This covers 4 squares (2 large, 8 small) it has 1 right angle but is the same length as next one it can be done twice (4). This shape is semectrical.

This covers 4 sq. (2 large 8 small). This one has no right angles but is the same length. 4 times.

You get 8 triangles out of these 2 triangles.

This can be done 8 times.

This can be done 16 times

This can be done 16 times.

This can be done 8 times. This one and the first triangle are the same area although.

This covers approx 2 sq (1 large 4 small) it can be done 4 times.

Keith (V.R.Q. 121)

There are 8 of these on a 9 pin board.

There are 4 of these on a 9 pin board.

25

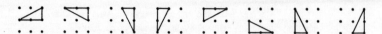

There are 16 of this size on a 9 pin board. Here are some.

These two triangles have the same area.

There are 4 of this size.

There are 16 of these

There are 4 (16) of this size on a 9 pin board.

These two are the same size. (Also same 'type' and repeat of previous triangles.)

These are both the same in area but not in shape.

Part 2
EXAMPLES OF ASSIGNMENT CARDS
Composed by Teachers

During the conferences held in July, 1968, for teachers from the Project's pilot areas, opportunity was given for those attending to devise assignment cards intended to serve different purposes in different situations. The cards were composed to come under one (or a combination of more than one) of the following headings:-

(a) *Situation dealt with:*

(i) one stemming from the pupils' own environment (whether natural or man-made);

(ii) one stemming from a pupil's familiarity with the circumstances of his own previous experience.

(b) *Type of assignments:*

(i) a long-term project, possibly involving a sequence of assignment cards;

(ii) a relatively short-term assignment (questions involving school work and homework, individual working and group working are relevant here).

(c) *Form of presentation of the assignment:*

(i) a clear cut, wholly or partially directed, format, for example the usual kind of multi-facet assignment card;

(ii) an open-ended format.

The assignment cards given below were selected from the large and varied quantity composed on these occasions. They are grouped under a few broad topic headings, and in some cases a sequence has been written into them by the composers. Apart from this, the situations depicted are not presented in any particular order, and this reflects what is sometimes a classroom procedure deliberately adopted by the teacher. Problem situations in real life do not by any means always come in a nicely ordered sequence, and the pupils may derive some useful experience from confronting changes of situation and having to adjust their thoughts accordingly.

An additional point might be made to support the choice of specimen assignments from this particular source. It shows that a considerable quantity and variety of assignments can be collected *quite quickly*, when a number of teachers combine together to produce them.

It must be stressed again that it is usually unhelpful to take up dogmatic attitudes of approval or otherwise of assignments designed by other people for other people's pupils and circumstances. The essential criterion is the pupils' response, and the final arbiter must be the teacher personally concerned with this. If this position is respected, it can then be mutually helpful for teachers to examine and discuss each other's assignment work. It is suggested that the following examples of cards be studied in this spirit. Their authors would not claim perfection of ideas or of phrasing. The pupils' reading of them would undoubtedly bring out the doubts and uncertainties which are so difficult to avoid in phrasing questions without becoming over-detailed and over pedantic.

A short introduction is given to each group of cards, but some points of general application can also be made:

1. Assignments directly relating to the Project's subject matter are, in many cases, written into its various books. This book is concerned with systems of assignments in general — their purposes, their diverse shapes, their compilation, and organisations for their use. Suggestions and ideas contained in it are available for consideration whether the subject matter involved is or is not derived directly from the Project's materials.

2. It has been suggested in the text that, if desired, assignment tasks could consist of direct numerical examples, of a familiar text-book pattern. It has not been thought necessary to include any of this type, but a study of the assignments below might include the consideration of what numerical response might emerge from them, in quality and quantity.

3. The teachers who composed the cards had certain pupils, or a certain ability range of pupils, in mind. It is worth remembering that many assignments could basically be used for pupils of different ages and abilities, given that they are re-phrased in sufficiently simple language for the pupils concerned, and that they require responses in suitable form — not necessarily in writing but possibly by word-of-mouth supported by diagram or apparatus.

4. This selection of cards in no way represents a 'course' of pupil material. It is hoped that they will show how much variety, of content and format, is possible, and that they will trigger off a wealth of further examples from the reader. The reader should consider such examples to be much better, insofar as his examples reflect his own experiences with his own pupils.

CARDS 1, 2, 3.

These three cards are all prompted by the view from a classroom window. The first two direct the pupil's attention to a variety of specific questions, Card 1 being of a genuine 'multi-facet' type in which the questions seek to introduce different 'facets' of mathematical ideas. Question 1 f may not appear at all reasonable if an answer were seriously expected: all the same it might be in accord with the atmosphere of a classroom in which some mathematical situations could lead to discussion and argument rather than to formal, written response.

The third card leaves the questioning much more open-ended: any or all of descriptive writing, diagrams, models and oral discussion could contribute to a pupil's answers.

Look through the window. You can see a large building. Look at the part which is made up of glass windows, blue panels, brown bricks and orange bricks.

a. How tall is it? (Measure your own height, then think of yourself standing at one of the windows.)

b. How long is it? (Measure your own pace, then think of yourself pacing its length.)

c. What is there most of? Blue panels, glass windows, orange brick strips or brown brick strips? Is the answer different if we think of (i) *numbers* of each (ii) total area of each sort separately?

d. Are all the lines parallel lines? Are they all parallel to each other? How many sets of parallel lines are there? Are there any important lines which are not members of any of these sets?

e. Suppose the building is made two stories higher. What happens to your answers to the above questions now?

f. If you had plenty of money, what sort of building made of the above materials would you make? Draw it. (Alternative: make a model of it.)

g. Suppose you had four glass windows, three long strips of dark bricks, six blue panels, and one long strip of orange bricks. How many different faces could your building have? Draw them. Which of them do you like best? Why? Which of them looks the strongest? Why? Which of them looks the weakest? Why?

h. Suppose someone tears each of your drawings in half down the middle. Which ones will give two halves which are the same? Are they *really* the same? In what way are they 'the same'? In what way are they 'not the same'?

CARD 2

Outside the window is a rectangular bed of shrubs of the same kind.

How many shrubs are there?
How long is the bed?
How many shrubs are planted along its length?
How wide is the bed?
How many shrubs are planted along its width?
How far apart are they measured along the length?
How far apart are they measured along the width?
About how many shrubs are planted to the square metre?
Could you check this result by measuring the area of the plot?
Measure the height of each plant as near as possible and record the number of plants of each height.
Now draw a graph showing the number of plants of each height.
Is there a pattern in your graph?

CARD 3

The wall of the building opposite is constructed from brick, has rows of rectangular windows and is partly lined with hexagonal tiles. Study the wall of the building immediately opposite. Can you see a pattern or patterns in the way the wall has been constructed? What shapes can you find in the patterns that you see? Sketch these patterns of shapes. A builder has to carry out work on this wall. What shape or shapes would he use to construct his scaffolding? Could you explain why he chose these shapes? If you cannot see the shapes that would be used, construct your own scaffolding from meccano strips. Cut out from card or lino tile the shapes that you have seen and by tracing around their edges try drawing patterns of tiles with each shape.

CARDS 4 (i to iii): 5 (i to iii): 6 (i to vi): 7 (i to vi)

These are four sets of cards composed as sequences of assignments. Some parts of the sequences are open-ended, some specifically directed.
The themes are:
Cards 4, shapes in the environment and their value for tessellations,
Cards 5, similarity and size in two and three dimensions,
Cards 6, quadrilaterals,
Cards 7, angular turn and angular measurements.

CARD 4(i)
1. Make a list of all the shapes you can discover outside the building.
2. If you are unable to describe them, sketch them.
3. Make an additional list of materials used in these shapes.

CARD 4(ii)
1. Suggest ways of setting out the information obtained from Card 4(i).
2. Put these on a sheet of paper or card using only the information you have already obtained.

CARD 4(iii)
Use pencil, ruler, compasses, card, coloured gummed paper and other material you choose.
1. Draw and cut out some of the shapes you have found.
2. See if any of the shapes can be used to cover completely a surface.
3. If you find any shapes that will fit, cut them out in coloured gummed paper to form a pattern.

CARD 5(i)
Take a tile in the shape of an equilateral triangle. Can you fit several of these together to make a triangle whose sides are twice as long? How many triangles did you use?
Can you make a triangle with sides three times as long?
Complete the table:

Length of side	No. of tiles
x 2	—
x 3	—

CARD 5(ii)

Take a match box. Using more match boxes make a cuboid, which is twice the size, three times the size, etc.

Complete the table:

No. of times the size	No. of match boxes

Draw a graph to show the relationship between the size and the number of matchboxes used.

Note. 'size' is measured here in terms of length, breadth and height.

CARD 5(iii)

Use the triangular tiles and make as many different shapes as possible.

Double the size of the sides of each shape in turn and count the number of triangles you have used to make each new shape.

CARD 6(i)

Take 4 straws of equal length.
Connect them by means of elastic (or pipe cleaners).
Keep your shape flat on the desk.
What shapes can you make?
When you alter the shape what happens to the perimeter?
When you alter the shape what happens to the area?
When you alter the shape what happens to the angles?
When is the area a maximum?

CARD 6(ii)

Take two small straws, of equal size, and two large straws of equal size. Thread them on your shirring elastic. Lay them flat on the desk. Move the shape about. What different shapes can you make?

What happens to perimeter, area and angles?

Have you threaded them in the only way possible? If not, re-thread them and see if any new shapes arise.

In how many different ways can you thread them?

CARD 6(iii)

Using four straws of any lengths make what shapes you can.

Can you always make a closed shape?

Can you make any new quadrilaterals?

How many sets or classes can you make?

CARD 6(iv)

Go around the school buildings and find any examples of these quadrilaterals.

Which shapes or shape occurs most often?

Can you suggest any reason or reasons for your findings?

CARD 6(v)

(1) Draw as large a square as you can and find the mid-point of each side.

(2) Join the mid-point of one side to the mid-point of the next side and so on until you have drawn a new shape.

(3) What is the new shape?

Using your *new* shape **repeat (1) and (2) above.**

Continue doing this until your 'new' shape is too small.

(4) Colour your finished pattern.

(5) What other patterns can you see in the large square?

(6) Now repeat this work starting with any four-sided figure.

CARD 6(vi)

Choose a quadrilateral and then draw a copy with the sides twice as big.

How many of the small ones will fit into the big one?

How many do you think would fit into a copy with sides three times as big?

CARD 7(i)

There are many things that we do that involve turning.

Sometimes you need a complete turn, sometimes half a turn, sometimes many turns. Below, you will find a list of tasks dealing with things that turn. Write out the amount of turn, or turns, needed for each of these.

1. The amount of turn to open your front door with a key.
2. The amount of turn needed to turn up the volume on your radio, to full.
3. The amount of turn needed to unscrew the top of a bottle of ink.
4. The amount of turn of the minute hand of a watch going from 11 o'clock to 12 o'clock.
5. The amount of turn of a bicycle wheel in travelling from one end of the yard to the other.

CARD 7(ii)

1. Walk around the outside of the yard, and make note of the amount of turn at each point where you change direction and add your answers together (in number of turns).
2. Do the same thing in the school hall.
3. Do the same thing in any other room in the school.
4. Do you notice anything about your answers?
5. Are the school yard, the school hall, and the 3rd room you used the same sizes?
6. What can you decide from your answers from 4 and 5?

CARD 7(iii)

Take one of the following questions and see what you can find out.

1. Draw a sketch map of your journey from home to school showing the amount of turns you make.

2. Go to the front entrance of the school, and pick out any large building you see. Say how you would direct a stranger to this building.

CARD 7(iv)

Devise a method of measuring the amount of turn on any shape with straight sides.

CARD 7(v)

You have been measuring turns.

Can you think of some ways of giving a more exact picture for 'bits of a turn'?

CARD 7(vi)

Look at Card 7(i).

Now use the method you have just devised to give these turns in terms of 'degrees'.

CARDS 8 and 9

Each of these cards has a specific teaching point in mind, and the questions lead the pupil towards this objective *by easy stages* — the technique of 'programmed learning'.

The particular aims are:

Card 8, the formula for the angle-sum of a polygon,

Card 9, a relationship between shapes and numbers of pins on a pinboard.

CARD 8

1. Draw a triangle. What is the sum of the angles?

2. Draw a quadrilateral. Draw in a diagonal. How many triangles are there in the figure? What is the sum of the interior angles of the quadrilateral?

3. Draw a pentagon. Draw in 2 diagonals from the same point. How many triangles are there in this figure? What is the angle sum of the pentagon?

4. Repeat this process with figures of 6, 7 .... 12 sides, remembering to draw the diagonals from any *one* point and making as many triangles as you can.

5. Tabulate the results in 3 columns under the headings:

(a) Number of sides of figure

(b) Number of triangles made

(c) Sum of interior angles of figure

6. What happens if the figure has n sides (n = any number)?

(i) How many triangles would be formed?

(ii) What is sum of angles in the figure? (You must use 'n' in your answer to this.)

7. What is *a* formula for finding the angle sum of any polygon?

A.

(i) On a pinboard mark out 8 shapes by putting bands around the pins while ensuring that there are *no* pins inside the shapes; find the area of each.

e.g.

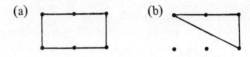

(a)   (b)

(ii) Copy and complete the following table:

	EXTERIOR NAILS (E)	AREA (A)
(a)	6	2 sq units
(b)	4	1 sq unit
etc.		

(iii) See if you can spot a rule connecting area and exterior nails and write it down in terms of A and E.

B.

(i) Mark out 8 shapes by putting the bands around the pins as before, but this time you can have pins on the inside; again find the area of each shape.

(ii) Copy and complete the following table:

	EXTERIOR PINS (E)	INTERIOR PINS (I)	AREA (A)
(a)	8	1	4 sq units
(b)	10	3	7 sq units
etc.			

(iii) Now see if you can spot the rule connecting A, E and I. Discuss among yourselves, then write it down.

CARD 10

This assignment seeks to probe the pupil's awareness of the significance of lines of symmetry. It would be interesting to see what variety of results might be obtained by *not* sketching lines of symmetry in the diagrams of part (a), and by *not* specifying the drawing of a line of symmetry as the first task in part (b).

CARD 10

Copy and complete the following unfinished figures so that they become symmetrical:

(a)

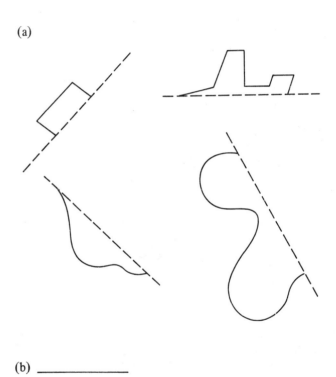

(b) _____

Draw a line of symmetry.

Within your group draw one half of a shape, and ask a member to complete the shape so that the whole is symmetrical.

CARDS 11, 12 and 13

These three cards approach, in different ways, some of the two-dimensional and three-dimensional problems involved in staircases, basing the situations on actual staircases on the premises. Card 12, in particular, might be considered more appropriate for eventual discussion rather than for written answers.

CARD 11

Consider the set of steps nearest to the Dining Room.
What is the 'rise' of one step?
How many of these steps would be needed to reach the roof?
What is the 'tread' of each step?
How far away from the Dining Room wall would the foot of the steps be?

CARD 12

The Science Block has a zig-zag staircase.
Try to think out reasons for this choice of design.
You might proceed as follows:
1. Make some rough sketches of some other designs.
2. Write down what you think each of your designs might involve.
3. What are your conclusions? Is the zig-zag a good or a bad design?
(The pupils might go on to consider why some buildings use lifts, and some escalators.)

CARD 13

Measure one of the steps leading up to the raised lawn outside the common room.
Make a half-scale drawing and use it to estimate the angle at which the grass bank is sloping.

CARDS 14 and 15

Each of these cards is aimed at a specific geometrical idea.

Card 14 deals with 'levelness', and offers the teacher a chance of discussing the more precise meanings of the words 'level', 'smooth', 'flat' and 'horizontal', which are commonly mixed up and used imprecisely by the man-in-the-street.

Card 15 can lead into the exploration of 'rolling' curves, such as the cycloid, epicycloid and hypocycloid. It can be linked with assignments concerned with gear wheels arising from the Project's book *Machines, Mechanisms and Mathematics*. And it can be supplemented with further assignments concerned with loci.

CARD 14

1. Find roughly level surfaces outside the school building, and list them in some way.

2. Are any of them 'exactly' level? Could you find more than one way of showing whether the surface was in fact 'exactly' level?

3. Of the surfaces that are not level, could you say how they are not level and show any differences in any practical way?

CARD 15

Cut out a cardboard circle of 5 cm radius. Mark the centre O, and a point on the circumference as P.

Sketch the path taken by O:

(a) When the circle is rolled along your desk top.

(b) When rolled around the *outside* edge of your exercise book.

(c) When rolled around the inside of a rectangular tray.

(d) When rolled around the outside of a 15 cm circle.

Can you now find what happens to P when you are doing questions (a) to (d)?

CARDS 16, 17, 18, 19, 20, 21, 22, 23

Practical, everyday problems are an obvious source of assignments, and a variety of these are dealt with in these eight cards: some concern the 'consumer', some the 'producer'.

The topics are:

Cards 16 and 23, shapes and sizes of household containers,

Card 17, do we pay for what we do not want? (this card has been criticised for dealing with an unrealistic situation: perhaps . . . but perhaps not?)

Card 18, fire insurance,

Card 19, comparison between 'sale' and 'original' prices; taken from real life some difficult quantities might emerge which could lead to a discussion on possible approximations,

Cards 20, 21, 22, designs and costs in building.

CARD 16

You will need a selection of 'containers', of different sizes and shapes and for different types of content, solid or liquid.

Compare the volume of the container with the surface area of material used.

Graph results.

From the graph, estimate the most efficient form of wrapping or container.

CARD 17

Your mother bought a 50 kg bag of coke which was wet because it had been raining for a week. She had another 50 kg bag which was very dry. They cost 50 p each.

(a) Which one would you rather buy?

(b) Why?

(c) Does water burn?

(d) How much a kilogramme was the coke in the first bag?

(e) How much a kilogramme was the coke in the second bag?

CARD 18

INSURANCE CLAIM

Unfortunately you have lost all your clothes in a fire at home. Fortunately the contents of the house were insured. Make a list of the clothes you possess and calculate the total cost of replacing them. Estimate as necessary. Make a table like this:

Item of Clothing	Number Owned	Cost of Replacing one	Cost of Replacing all

Total Cost ━━━━━━━━━━━━━━▶

CARD 19

From newspapers, hoarding boards, shop-windows, advertisements:

(a) find the original cost

(b) find the sale price of different articles of varying price range (cheap, expensive)

(i) Find the amount of reduction in each case;

(ii) Which article gives the best bargain? The one with the greatest amount of reduction in price? (Discuss)

(iii) What fraction of the original price in each case has been 'knocked off'? By looking at these fractions can you decide which is the largest (i.e. greatest) reduction? (Discuss)

(iv) Change these fractions to percentages and again compare. Which looks the 'best buy' now?

CARD 20

A plot of ground of dimensions 10 m by 27m is purchased.

1. Draw a plan of a bungalow using approximately ½ of the plot of ground. The rest of the ground is used up in paths, pond, garage and lawns.

2. Put in a circular pond 2 m in diameter.

3. Put in a garage 6 m by 3 m.

4. Put in the necessary paths 60 cm wide.

5. What proportion of the plot is lawn?

6. Are you satisfied with your plan?

7. Could you improve this plan? If so, do so and state your reason for doing so.

CARD 21

1. Measure the hall floor, and draw a plan to scale.
2. Make a sketch to show the pattern in which the blocks are laid down.
3. How many blocks are used in covering the floor?
4. At a cost of ten new pence per block, find the price of the blocks used?
5. Is there another way of arranging the blocks so that a smaller number is used.
6. Draw a sketch to show your new pattern.
7. Why do you think the blocks have been laid as they are?

CARD 22

Find out the number of bricks used in building your house.

Find the weight of one brick. What is the total weight of bricks needed for one house?

If all these bricks are stacked together, how much space will they occupy?

Find out the area of the floor of a three-ton lorry.

How many bricks will cover the floor of the lorry?

How many bricks could safely be carried in one three-ton lorry?

How many lorries would be required to carry the bricks for one house?

(which is similar to, but significantly different
from Card 16)

Bottles

Find out some facts about various kinds of bottles and their contents.

These bottles could be:

  (i) sauce bottles of all kinds;

 (ii) sauce bottles of a particular kind (e.g. tomato ketchup);

(iii) bottles of shampoo.

Find out, either

  (1) from bottles you have at home;

  (2) from bottles in friends' homes; or

  (3) by visits to shops:

(a) the height of the bottles (in cm)

(b) the amount of the contents (cu cm)

(c) the cost of the bottle and its contents.

Draw a graph showing height and amount of contents.

(a) Does there seem to be any connection between these quantities?

(b) Would you expect any connection?

(c) Does there seem to be an exact connection? (relationship?)

       a rough connection?

       no connection?

Draw a graph showing amount of contents and price.

(d) What lines could you draw in order to show the relative cheapness or otherwise of the contents?

What other considerations might you take into account if you were buying one of these things?

CARDS 24, 25, 26, 27, 28

These cards present assignments concerned with statistics. The technique of a 'social survey' is introduced, together with ideas of sampling and frequency. The Project's book *Luck and Judgement* offers a wide variety of assignments based on problems of probability and statistics.

CARD 24

Make a questionnaire on the type of heating that is used at home. Circulate these among your class.

Collect and show the results in as many different ways as you can and write a short account of your findings.

(Extensions:

To whole school community.

Comparison of small group results as against whole community results.

Compare types of house and types of heating.)

CARD 25

1. Bring to school a copy of as many newspapers as possible.

2. Read the leader article in any two — preferably a 'posh paper' and a 'popular' one.

3. Make a frequency count of the 2, 3, 4, etc. lettered words in the first 500 words of each article.

4. Make a frequency histogram of each result (a) separately (b) superimposing the one upon the other.

5. Do you notice anything about the shapes of the two graphs?

6. What does this suggest about the typical reader of the 'posh' and 'popular' papers?

7. Repeat, using different newspapers, periodicals. Similarly, compare the word choice of different authors (e.g. Jane Austen and Ian Fleming).

CARD 26

Choose any book from the library.

Find the thickness of each page.

Choose any page. Count the number of words on any line.

Count the number of lines on the page.

How many words would you expect to find on the page?

How many words are there on the page?

Approximately how many words are there in the book?

Find the frequency of each letter of the alphabet on the page you have chosen.

Draw a histogram from your results.

Examine the key-board of a typewriter and a typing manual.

List the letters to be typed by each digit.

Is there any relation between the position of the keys and the frequency of the letters?

How do you think the typewriter keys could be best arranged?

CARD 27

Site of work .... the beach.

Tasks:

(1) Collect 200 pebbles (a) 'Along' the beach; (b) On a line at right angles to the tide mark.

(2) Make measurements of these pebbles, record your facts and draw histograms to illustrate your findings.

Question: Are your collections good samples?

CARD 28

It has been stated in a newspaper that only 20% of drivers obey the built-up area speed limit. Test the truth of this statement.

CARDS 29, 30, 31, 32, 33, 34, 35.

Car parking offers many chances for assignments, whether geometrical or statistical. These seven cards exploit such opportunites in varying ways. Not only are there differences in the types of pupil investigation available from this topic, but there are differences in the ways in which data and conclusions can be presented — e.g. descriptions, tabulations, various alternative forms of diagram, oral discussion.

CARD 29

1. Walk round the campus and study each car; complete the undermentioned tables with respect to each car.

2. Represent the results obtained in A and B graphically in as many ways as possible.

3. Summarize your results in your books.

A – MAKES

AUSTIN	FORD	MORRIS	VAUXHALL			etc.

B–COLOURS

BLACK	WHITE	L' BLUE	D' BLUE	GREEN	TWO TONE	etc,

CARD 30

(a) How many cars are there on the car park?
(b) Write down registration numbers.
(c) Find any groups or patterns or sets in these numbers.
(d) Present this information in as many ways as possible.

CARD 31

(a) Collect colours, makes and registration numbers of cars on the car park.

(b) How could you present this information?

CARD 32
VEHICLE CENSUS

1. Visit car parks in your vicinity.
2. Record types and registration number of all vehicles.
3. From A.A. book find which county all vehicles come from.
4. List all counties. How many cars come from each?
5. Why do more people come from some counties than others?
6. How many of the cars are one year old?
   How many of the cars are two years old?
   How many of the cars are three years old?
   How many of the cars are four years old?
   How many of the cars are five years old?
   How many of the cars are over five years old?
7. Display this information on a pie-chart.

CARD 33
GO TO THE CAR PARK AND LOOK AT THE CARS

A. How many cars are there altogether?
   What percentage have four doors?
B. Fords claim that 3 out of 5 cars are made by them.
   Do the cars in the car park bear this out?
C. How many saloon cars are there?
   What percentage have roofs that can be opened?
D. How many cars are:
   (a) over four (4) years old?
   (b) under four (4) years old?
   Are seat belts more likely to be found in new cars than in old cars?

and two examples of 'planning' car parks:

You are going to find out how many cars can be parked in the car park.

You will need:

A Surveyor's tape, coloured card, and a sheet of plain or squared paper.

Solve the problem this way:

1. Measure the area available for parking.

2. Do a scale drawing of the car park, using a convenient scale, and using squared paper if you think this is helpful.

3. Find the length and width of a normal large car. Add 1 metre to the length and 120 cm to the width to give the size of a parking place. (Does this seem reasonable to you?)

4. On the coloured card draw and cut out such rectangles to the same scale as the drawing of the car park. Each rectangle represents a parking place. They can be arranged side by side but not usually end to end.

5. Arrange your coloured rectangles on your scale drawing of the car park, allowing space to drive in and out. When you have a good layout stick the rectangles down, and write how many cars can be parked there.

CARD 35

In a hundred metre stretch of road, how many cars can be parked:

(a) end to end?

(b) side by side?

Draw scale diagrams to show how you would set out parking lines. When could you not use one of the above methods?

(Possibility of pupils using toys for the investigation could lead on to a study of car turning circles.)

CARDS 36, 37, 38, 39, 40, 41

If what are loosely designated as topics of 'modern mathematics' form part of a pupil's studies, assignments can be as readily drawn from them as from any other source.

These six cards refer to:

Binary systems of measurement   (Card 36)
Punched-card systems   (Card 37)
Matrices   (Cards 38 and 39)
Vectors   (Card 40)
Topology   (Card 41)

CARD 36
(Binary scale measurement)

Measure the length of your foot to the nearest cm and then fill out the table below:

No. of foot lengths	1	2	4	8	16
No. of cm					

Using *ONLY* the values in the table above, calculate the number of cm in the following foot lengths:

(a) 3   (b) 15   (c) 5   (d) 7   (e) 30   (f) 24.

Using the set of 1 lb, 2 lb, 4 lb, and 8 lb weights, weigh out the following amounts of sand:

(a) 6 lb   (b) 10 lb   (c) 13 lb   (d) 14 lb.

Can a shop keeper get away with using just such a set of weights if he only has to weigh whole pounds up to 15 lb? Suppose a shop keeper only had the weights 1 lb, 3 lb, and 9 lb, could he weigh out the following quantities?:

(a) 2 lb   (b) 4 lb   (c) 7 lb   (d) 10 lb.

Try it out!!

Each pupil has a postcard, with a line of holes punched along an edge, and puts his name on the card.

The holes are numbered from 1 upwards, from right to left. The leader asks the following questions; if the answer is *yes* a slot is made down from edge to hole; if it is *no* the card is not touched.

$$\text{o o o o o o o o}$$
$$8\ 7\ 6\ 5\ 4\ 3\ 2\ 1$$

(Example: if your answer to question 1 is *yes* then your card should look like this: if *no* leave hole as it is.)

Questions:
1. Have you any brothers?
2. Are you a boy?
3. Have you any sisters?
4. Are you a girl?
5. Is your hair fair?
6. Is your hair dark?
7. Are you more than 5 ft 5 in in height?
8. Do you walk to school?
9. Do you ride a bicycle to school?
10. Do you ride in a bus to school?

$$\text{o o o o o o o}$$
$$8\ 7\ 6\ 5\ 4\ 3\ 2\ 1$$

(A cut off corner helps in placing the cards the right way.)

Let us find out who (if anybody):
(i) has no brothers
(iii) is male
(v) has dark hair
(ii) has no sisters
(iv) less than 5 ft 5 in
(vi) rides a bus to school.

How is this done? Is the 'result' correct? Make up some similar questions of your own, and so identify members of the class.

A motorist calls at a garage and collects 4 gallons of petrol and one pint of oil. Represent this by $\begin{pmatrix} 4 \\ 1 \end{pmatrix}$

A second motorist gets 3 gallons of petrol and 2 pints of oil. Represent this in a similar way.

How much petrol and oil has been sold altogether?

Represent this: $\begin{pmatrix} 4 \\ 1 \end{pmatrix}$ followed by $\begin{pmatrix} 3 \\ 2 \end{pmatrix} \longrightarrow \begin{pmatrix} \\ \end{pmatrix}$.

How would you represent: 2 gallons of petrol, no oil
                        no petrol, 2 pints of oil?

A motorist collects 5 gallons of petrol and 3 pints of oil in some containers. On finding that these are the wrong grades he returns them to the garage.

Represent these actions (and the final result).

Consider this kind of representation for (say) 5 items in a supermarket.

(On previous cards the possibilities of the uses of matrices have been explored.)

Try your new knowledge on these situations.

1. Yesterday John went to the school shop and bought four 1p Kit-Kats and two 2p Oxo crisps. Susan bought five Kit-Kats and three Oxo crisps.

Write down the appropriate quantity matrix and price vector showing this.

Hence, find the amount of money each spend at the shop.

2. Plot and join up these points on your graph paper (1,1) (4,1) (4,3). Operate the transformation matrix $\begin{pmatrix} 0 & 1 \\ -1 & 0 \end{pmatrix}$

on these points. Plot your new points on the graph paper and join up.

What effect has this operation had on the original shape?

Map of Majority Isle

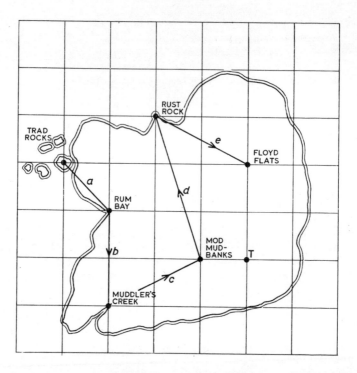

Your ship founders on Trad Rocks just off the treacherous island of Child Beaters. Your wanderings include vectors *a, b, c, d, e,* which are in the senses shown on the chart.

(i) Give the numerical value, in column form of each of these vectors, *a, b, c, d, e.*

(ii) What is the vector Mod Mudbanks to Floyd Flats?

(iii) What is the value, in column form, of vector addition *a + b + c*?

(iv) From Mod Mudbanks you follow vectors *d + (−e)*. What is your vector back to shipwreck on Trad Rocks?

(v) What is vector sum *b + c + d + e*?

(vi) You find treasure at the point T. What is the vector from T to Muddler's Creek direct?

A hypothetical topological problem, which could be applied to the actual lay-out of the pupil's school:

You are now in Classroom X.

In the event of a fire you must go to a point Y in the playground.

What is your best route in each of these cases:
(i) The fire is not in a position to impede you;
(ii) The fire is in Classroom Z, which is on the route taken in (i);
(iii) The boys and girls in Classroom Z *have* to take a certain route from Z to Y, and you must not be on this route at all.
Can you represent these alternatives simply on a diagram?
In making this diagram, do the distances and directions of the various routes matter to you?

CARDS 42, 43, 44, 45, 46
A mixture of oddments!

Card 42, a lead into ideas of limits and infinity,
Card 43, an interesting numerical device, suggesting some algebraic generalisation.

Both these cards have been criticised as being of far too great difficulty for the pupils with whom the Project is concerned. This would certainly be true if they were set as formal questions for formal answering. But they could each have interest-value for discussion — maybe in the context of a 'mathematics club'. The idea of numerical limiting values contained in Card 42 might appropriately be linked with ideas of geometrical limiting positions which pupils had come across in loci and envelopes (e.g. in curve-stitching techniques) or in relationship graphs that involved hyperbolas (e.g. the law of the lever, and constant-area rectangles).
Card 43 might include discussion on —
(a) Is there a distinction between 'useful' and 'valid'? and
(b) What happens in 'awkward cases' — if the number to be squared is less than 25?

Card 44, a practical situation in furniture design, involving conflicts between mechanical possibility and good sense,
Card 45, an example of arithmetic motivated by recreation,
Card 46, a long-term assignment, depending for its development on

day-to-day observations. This could lead to discussion about the interpretation of 'recording' — with some pupils evolving some sort of
diagrammatic representation of the measurements, while others might try
to sketch a 'picture'. And will tabulation involve (as the composer of the
assignment planned) a use of negative numbers?

CARD 42
(A lead into 'limits' and 'infinity')

Do the following sums in order:

$\frac{10}{1} =$, $\frac{10}{0.1} =$, $\frac{10}{0.01} =$, $\frac{10}{0.001} =$,

$\frac{10}{0.0001} =$; $\frac{10}{0.00001} =$, $\frac{10}{0.000001} =$,

What do you notice about your answers as you do your sums?

What do you notice about each denominator?

Complete a statement such as this: 'As my divisor becomes
.... my answer becomes ....

CARD 43
(An interesting numerical situation, suggesting some algebraic
generalisation.)

Practise using the following rule for squaring numbers:
To square 47:
1. Take 47 from 50 and square the answer, writing the result as
two digits (if necessary using a zero as a place holder); result = 09.
2. Take 25 from 47 giving 22;
Then $47^2 = 2209$.
Between what limits is this a *useful* short cut?

(Pupils might investigate this algebraically.)

56

CARD 44

(An assignment involving conflicts between mechanical possibilities and good sense!)

1. Why do most tables have four legs?
2. Is it possible to have a table with (a) 1 leg? (b) 2 legs? (c) 3 legs?
3. If the table top is round, where would one leg best be placed?
4. If the table is square, where would one leg best be placed?
5. If the table is rectangular where would one leg best be placed?
6. What would be the answers to questions 3, 4 and 5:
   (a) .... if the table had two legs?
   (b) .... if the table had three legs?

CARD 45

Do you know how to play darts? If not, find out and make sure you know how to score before you answer these questions.

Remember that you must start with a double and finish with a double exactly.

1. (a) Your total near the end of the game is 36. Your 3 darts score 10, 7, double 9. Have you won?

(b) Give 2 ways in which you could finish exactly from 36.

2. (a) Your total is 200. Your 3 darts score 6, double 8, 25. What is your total now?

(b) Your next 3 darts score double 15, 16, treble 20. What is your score now?

(c) How could you finish next time?

3. If you are not very good at darts it would be safest to aim at the part of the board where three neighbouring numbers have the highest total, (for example 5 and 1 are next to 20, so the total here is 26.) Where would be the best place to aim?

4. What would be the fewest number of darts needed to finish a game of 301, beginning and ending with a double? Give the score of each dart.

CARD 46

Put blotting paper round the inside of a jar and fill with slightly damp sand. Between the blotting paper and the glass, and half way down the jar, place (on opposite sides of the jar) a pea and a bean. Water until the blotting paper changes colour.

After watering daily watch what is happening, and record the measurements of any shoots and roots on graph paper, as suggested here:

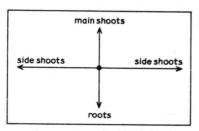

Tabulate the results throughout the period of observed growth.